Diving Deep

Using Machines to Explore the Ocean

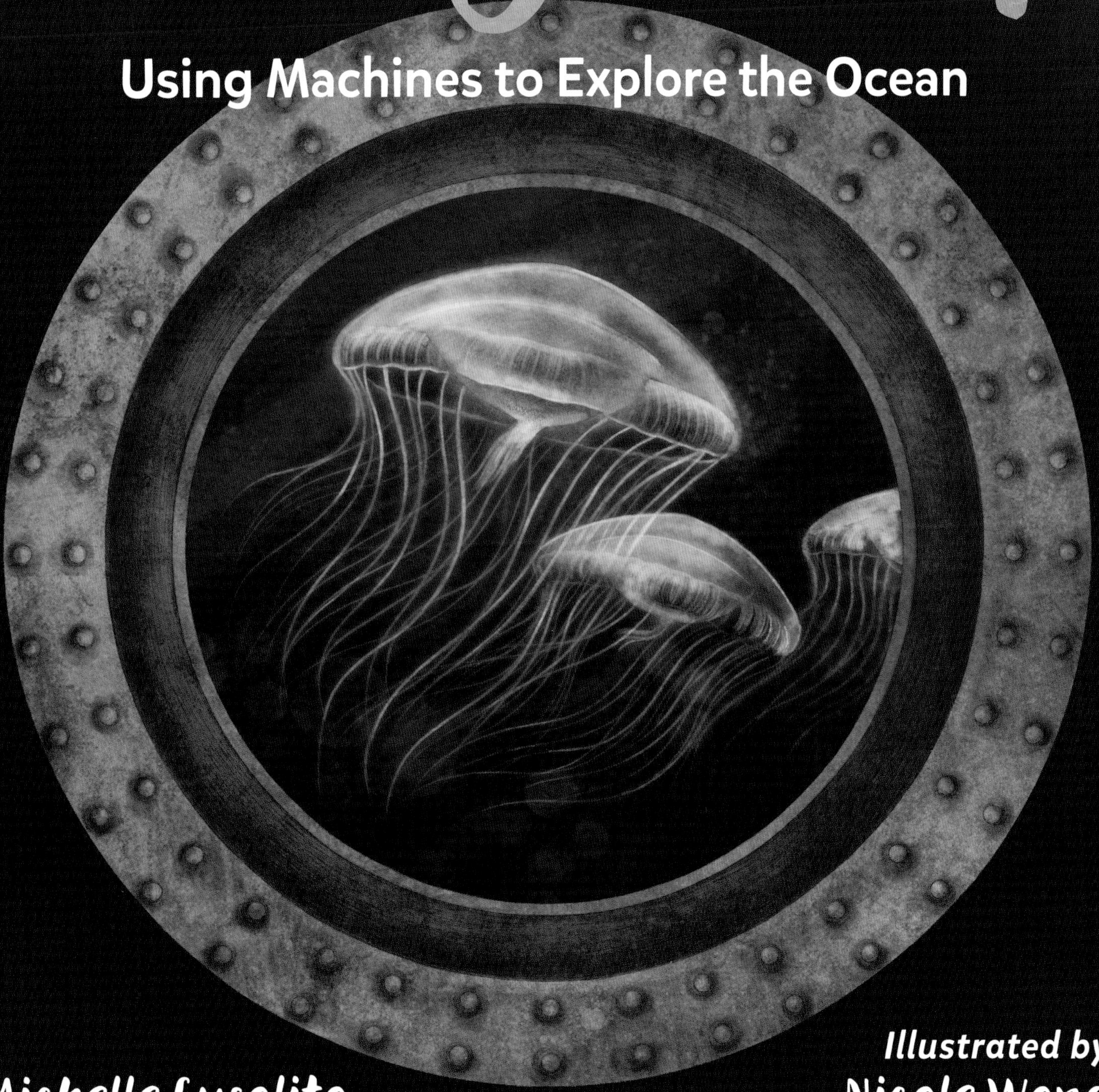

Michelle Cusolito

Illustrated by
Nicole Wong

Charlesbridge

Far away from shore,
past beaches and coral reefs,
the ocean's surface conceals
Earth's last unexplored wilderness.

What drives humans to dive into the sea
and sink deeper than the last inkling of light?

We're wired for wonder.
We delight in discovery.

For some,
danger is the draw.
Others chase the thrill
of an unseen seascape—
to confront the unknown
and push the limits of exploration.

We strive to unlock the ocean's secrets.

We dive deep.

We swim with fins and breathe through tubes. We glimpse angelfish hiding among sea fans and eavesdrop on parrotfish crunching on corals.

SNORKELING

Maximum depth: about a meter (a few feet)
Time: until the swimmer is tired or cold
Number of people: at least 2 for safety

Swimmers keep their faces submerged and breathe through a snorkel—a tube attached to a mask. The mask enables swimmers to see. Anyone who knows how to swim can learn to snorkel. There isn't much danger involved.

We hold our breath and strain our bodies to dive deeper and longer than once thought possible. We swim among sperm whales and feel their clicks vibrate through our bones and chests.

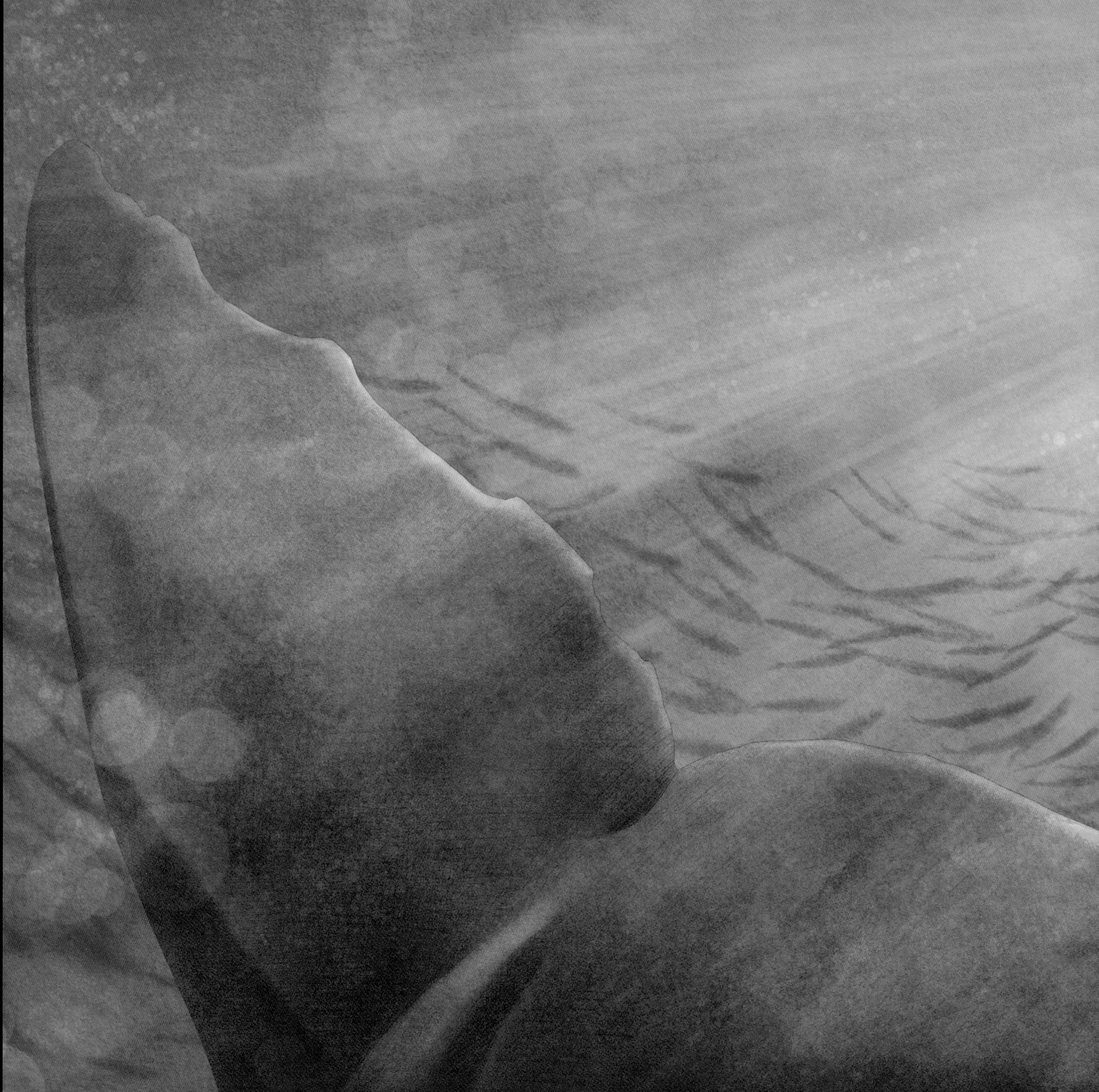

Freediving

Typical depth: 30 meters (about 100 feet)
Dive time: usually 1 to 2 minutes per dive
Number of people: at least 2 for safety

Freedivers train to dive on a single breath of air. Most freedivers wear a wet suit so they can stay warm and relaxed. When studying or photographing animals, they use a snorkel so they can return to the surface to breathe while keeping their eyes on animals below. As freedivers descend, their heart rates slow. Blood rushes inward from their arms and legs to protect their organs, and their lungs shrink from the pressure of the water. The biggest risk is divers pushing beyond their limits and drowning. Safety divers remain at the surface, ready to assist if someone needs help.

Scuba diving

Recreational depth: 40 meters (about 130 feet)
Time: usually 30 to 50 minutes
Number of people: at least 2 for safety

The word scuba comes from "self-contained underwater breathing apparatus." Scuba divers breathe compressed air from a tank. People age ten and up can become certified scuba divers. Divers use dive tables or a dive computer to determine how deep they can go and how long they can safely stay at depth. Gases accumulate in a diver's bloodstream from breathing compressed air and can bubble inside the body if a diver rises to the surface too quickly. Dive planning and a slow return to the surface help to avoid decompression sickness (DCS, or "the bends"). At a minimum, DCS is painful. At its worst, it can be life threatening.

We don fins and masks and strap air tanks onto our backs. We fly among fishes and spy on an octopus in its den.

We live in an underwater habitat for ten days or more, breathing steamy, compressed air. We dine by the viewport while a frowning goliath grouper stares through the glass.

Saturation diving

Lab depth: 15 meters (about 50 feet)

Dive depth outside lab: 12 to 28 meters (about 40 to 100 feet)

Time: about 10 days

Number of people: 6

Aquarius Reef Base, an underwater lab located off the coast of Florida, is slightly bigger than a city bus. Scientists who live and work in Aquarius dive to the lab using scuba gear. They live at two and a half times the pressure at sea level. Observers at the surface monitor the habitat through live video and audio feeds. By living at depth, scientists can dive for many more hours than from a boat on the surface, and they can complete research projects in less time. Before returning to the surface, they go through seventeen hours of decompression inside Aquarius. Then they swim to the surface using a small tank of air. Dangers include Aquarius system failure or DCS during quick emergency returns to the surface.

We put on a submarine suit with backpack thrusters and soar along the seafloor. We stop and walk on the bottom to collect specimens and photograph new species of bioluminescent animals.

Atmospheric diving suits

Maximum depth: 300 meters (about 1,000 feet)
Time: about 5 hours
Number of people: 1

An Exosuit is a wearable submarine that flies through the water. The pilot breathes air from a tank, and the hard suit protects them from the pressure. They use foot pedals to control thrusters that push them along. The suit is connected to the surface by a fiber-optic tether for two-way communication and live video feed. The pressure inside the suit is the same as at sea level, so the pilot can return to the surface without having to decompress. Dangers include system failure or entanglement.

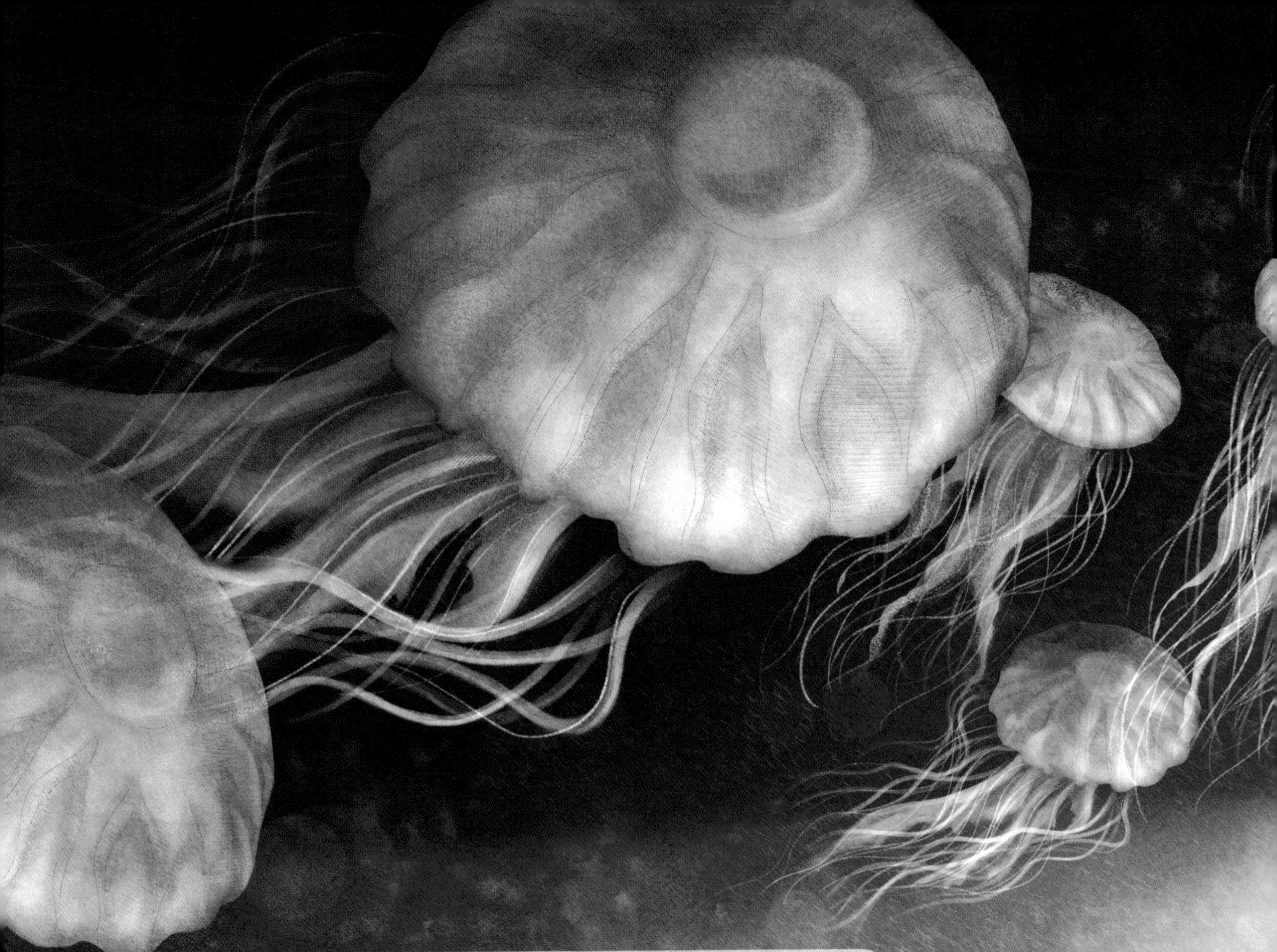

Deep-Diving Submersibles

Typical depth: up to 1,000 meters (3,300 feet)
Time: 6 to 12 hours
Number of people: 1 to 3

A DeepWorker submersible is like a chair with a submarine wrapped around it. As with other submersibles, the pressure inside is the same as at sea level. A clear domed top provides a wide view, and dives last about six hours. The pilot drives with their feet, leaving their hands free to take notes or photographs. A headset allows communication with the surface. Triton 3300 submersibles carry one to three people and can dive for up to twelve hours.

We pretzel ourselves into the cockpit of a submersible and descend to the ocean twilight zone, where little sunlight reaches. We observe the largest animal migration on Earth as a wave of sea jellies and small animals moves up to the sunlit zone.

We settle into a small space to spend all day peering into the dark, vast ocean through plate-sized viewports. We seek evidence that life on Earth began in the deep ocean.

Deeper-Diving submersibles

Maximum depth: 6,500 meters (21,325 feet)
Time: about 9 hours
Number of people: 3

Alvin is the longest continuously operating submersible in the world. It carries one pilot and two scientists. Pilots undergo intensive training and are certified by the US Navy. From its launch in 1964 through 2020, *Alvin* completed more than 5,000 dives and carried 3,021 different people to the seafloor. *Shinkai 6500* also carries three people: two pilots and one researcher. From 1989 to 2020, it completed more than 1,500 dives and carried more than a thousand different people. A thick metal sphere keeps people safe from intense deep-sea pressure. One of the biggest dangers is entanglement in anchor chains or fishing nets, which could prevent a safe return to the surface.

We tuck ourselves into a tiny sphere inside a submersible and plunge to the deepest, most perilous place on the planet: Challenger Deep. We could be the first humans to see species that have lived here for millions of years.

The deepest dive

Maximum depth: 10.9 kilometers (6.8 miles)

Time: 11 to 12 hours

Number of people: 1 to 2

Until 2019, only three people had been to Challenger Deep. Located in the Pacific Ocean, it's the deepest known place on Earth. Jacques Piccard and Don Walsh made the historic first dive in the *Trieste* in 1960. More than fifty years later, in 2012, filmmaker and explorer James Cameron torpedoed to Challenger Deep in *Deepsea Challenger*. Then, in 2019, Victor Vescovo dove to Challenger Deep in *Limiting Factor*. More people have since made the trip in *Limiting Factor*, including astronaut Dr. Kathy Sullivan in 2020. She's the first person to both walk in space and dive to Challenger Deep. These deepest dives are dangerous, but a thick metal sphere protects the passengers from the crushing pressure and careful engineering helps manage the risks.

The ocean is wild and dangerous and deep.
Why do we take such risks?

We're wired for wonder.
We delight in discovery.

We're ocean detectives
solving the mysteries of the deep,
and there's so much left to uncover.

Yesterday we found
a new species of shark
near the Galápagos Islands.

Today we explore
a lush landscape
deep below Antarctic ice.

Tomorrow we may
unlock more secrets of life on Earth.

And so . . .

. . . we dive deep.

Diving Deep

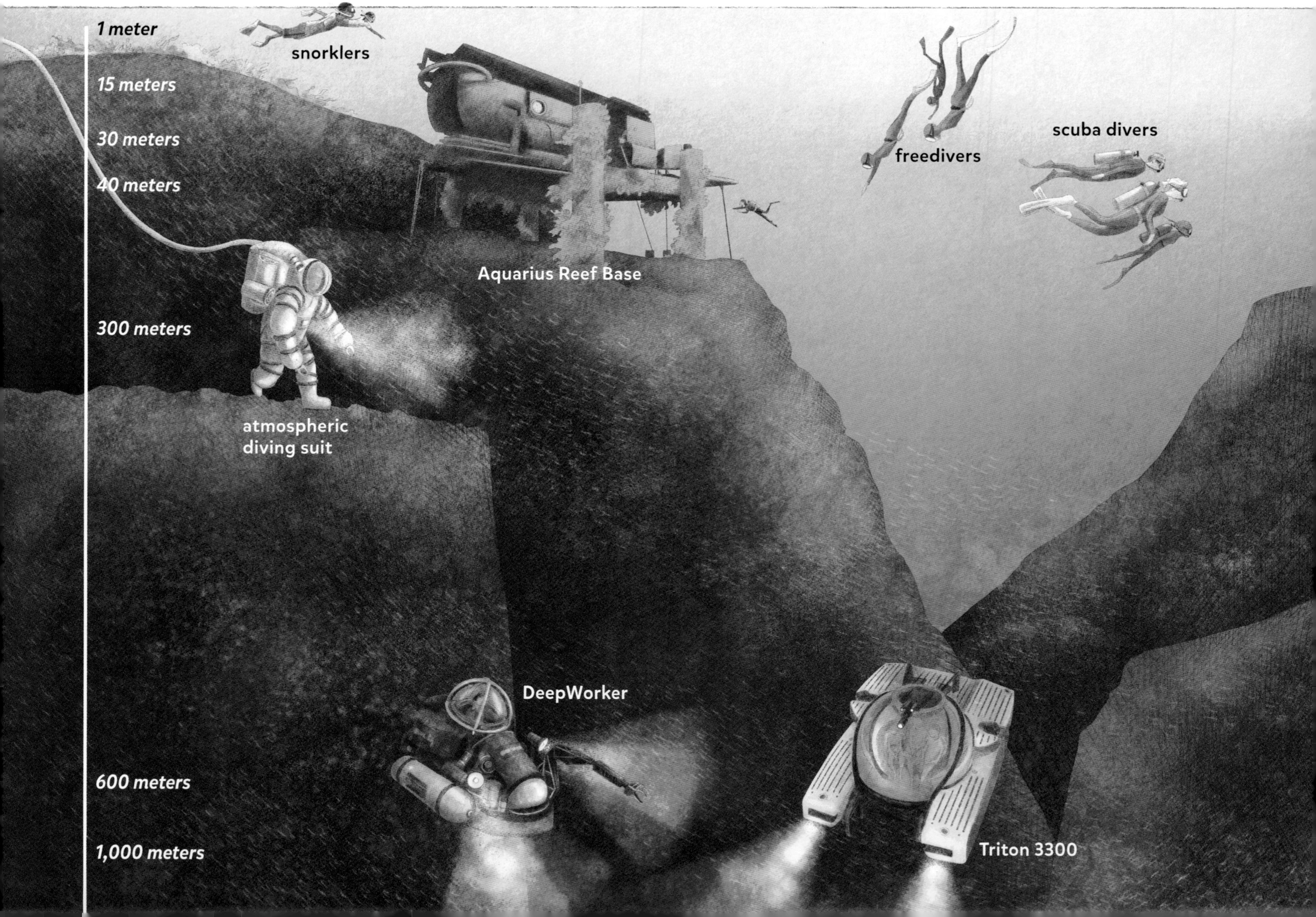
1 meter
snorklers
15 meters
30 meters
40 meters
Aquarius Reef Base
freedivers
scuba divers
300 meters
atmospheric
diving suit
DeepWorker
600 meters
1,000 meters
Triton 3300

The deeper we go into the ocean, the greater the pressure, or force, pushing on us. Pressure can be measured in units called atmospheres. Water pressure at sea level is 1 atmosphere. For every 10 meters (about 33 feet) of depth in the ocean, pressure increases by 1 more atmosphere. By the time you reach Challenger Deep at the bottom of the Mariana Trench, the pressure is a whopping 1,072 atmospheres. That would be like having fifty jumbo jets stacked on top of one person! (Note that the depths on this page aren't to scale. We'd need the page to be a lot longer for that!)

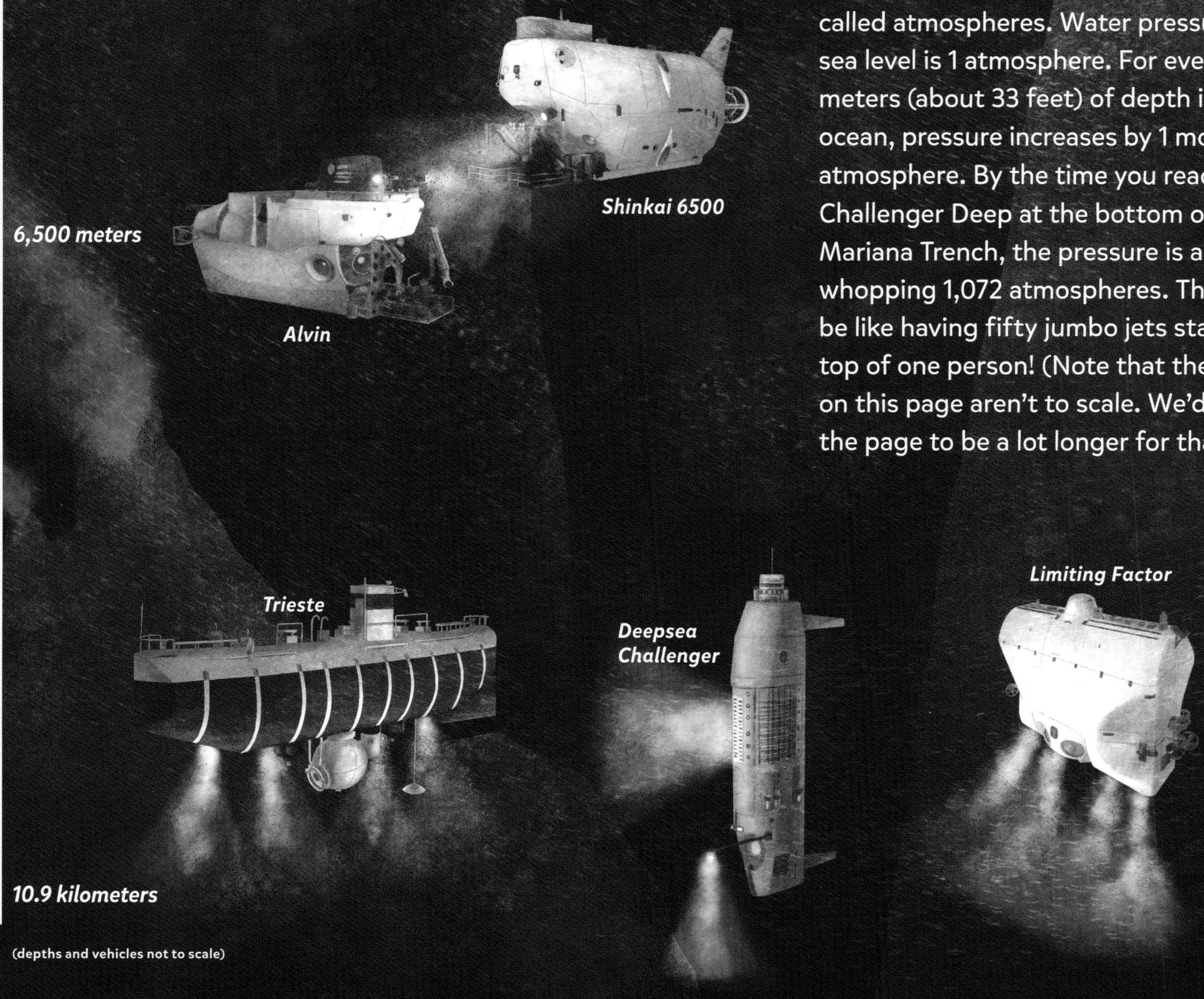

(depths and vehicles not to scale)

Author's Note

When I have an idea for a book, I usually do as much research as I can before contacting an expert. In this case, I first got the idea for this book when I was finishing another picture book, *Flying Deep: Climb Inside Deep-Sea Submersible ALVIN*. Bruce Strickrott, chief *Alvin* pilot and the manager of the Alvin Group, showed me a book that features machines designed by Leonardo da Vinci. Bruce and I agreed that a book about the variety of ways that humans travel deeper and deeper into the ocean would be valuable.

I wanted this book to be about the awe and wonder humans have for the ocean and the technologies we've designed that enable us to explore it. I chose to focus on the diving we do to expand scientific knowledge, research, and communication. That means I left out saturation diving for the oil industry, competitive freediving, and submarines designed for military or surveillance purposes.

Early technological advances led to the submersibles we now use for deep-ocean research. Every advancement in technology feeds more advancements. Jacques-Yves Cousteau is widely considered the father of underwater ocean exploration. He dedicated his life to expanding our knowledge of the ocean. He and Emile Gagnon invented modern scuba equipment in 1943. The Exosuit wouldn't be possible without the suits that came before it. There was the Newtsuit, the JIM suit, and so on. Engineers learn from each development and use that knowledge to improve future designs. As a result, new technologies are constantly emerging.

The first humans to visit the twilight zone were Otis Barton and William Beebe in 1930. They dove in the *Bathysphere*, a 1.4 meter (4.6 foot) metal sphere, lowered 244 meters (800 feet) on a tether. This historic dive paved the way for future deep-ocean exploration. Another groundbreaking dive came in 1960, when Don Walsh and Jacques Piccard dove 10.9 kilometers (6.8 miles) deep in *Trieste*. *Trieste*'s 2.2 meter (7.1 foot) metal sphere was suspended below a giant tank filled with gasoline. Gasoline floats and doesn't compress like gases do, so it provided the buoyancy needed to return once they dropped weight at the bottom. There are additional retired submersibles, such as *Mir I* and *Mir II*. These vessels facilitated important scientific research and led to engineering advancements that informed the development and improvement of other submersibles.

A Note About Measurements

Scientists around the world work in metric, which is why measurements in this book are in metric first with US measurements in parentheses. The conversions are sometimes rounded up or down because that's what divers do. For example, the sidebar about freediving says "30 meters (about 100 feet)." Really, 30 meters equals 98.4252 feet, but divers using US measurements round up and say 100 feet.

Glossary

apparatus: A group of tools or instruments used for a specific purpose, such as for diving.

bioluminescent: Describes a living thing that makes its own light.

buoyancy: The ability to float.

compressed: Squeezed into less space.

decompression sickness (DCS, or "the bends")**:** When divers breathe compressed air, gases such as nitrogen dissolve in their bloodstream. If they ascend (return to the surface) too quickly, the nitrogen bubbles as it leaves the blood. So divers return to the surface slowly. Saturation divers who go very deep or stay at depth for a long time need to decompress for a longer period of time. Imagine a shaken bottle of soda. If you open it right away, it will explode. Instead, you can open it slightly until you see bubbles forming, and then close it again. Wait a bit and repeat until you can safely open it. That's sort of what divers do when they control how quickly they return to the surface.

sphere: A ball or globe shape.

sunlit zone: The top layer of the ocean, where sunlight reaches. The sunlit zone is from the ocean's surface to about 200 meters (656 feet). Most seafood comes from this layer.

twilight zone: The layer of ocean where very little light reaches, between about 200 meters (656 feet) and 1,000 meters (3,300 feet). Plants cannot live here because there isn't enough light.

Learn More

Visit author Michelle Cusolito's website for additional resources at **www.michellecusolito.com.**

Books

Cusolito, Michelle. *Flying Deep: Climb Inside Deep-Sea Submersible ALVIN*. Watertown, MA: Charlesbridge, 2018.

Keating, Jess. *Ocean Speaks: How Marie Tharp Revealed the Ocean's Biggest Secret*. New York: Tundra Books, 2020.

Rosenstock, Barb. *Otis and Will Discover the Deep: The Record-Setting Dive of the Bathysphere*. New York: Little, Brown Books for Young Readers, 2018.

Videos

(Note: The URLs listed here were accurate at publication, but websites often change. If a URL doesn't work, you can use the internet to find more information.)

Watch remarkable 360-degree footage of whales and dolphins, taken by free divers. **http://www.darewin.org/page6**

Learn more about Aquarius. **https://environment.fiu.edu/aquarius/about**

A short review of earlier submersibles and a demonstration of how DeepWorker is piloted, plus an interview with ocean pioneer Sylvia Earle. **https://www.youtube.com/watch?v=tRd612BrDKU**

To Dante, who shares my endless curiosity about the world, and Alia, who helps me find the best way to write about it
—M. C.

For Kathleen and Millie
—N. W.

Special thanks to Bruce Strickrott, chief *Alvin* pilot and *Alvin* Group manager, for inspiring this book and for providing expert guidance along the way. Thank you to the following experts: Captain Philip G. Renaud, USN (Ret.), program manager of the Ocean Twilight Zone Project at Woods Hole Oceanographic Institution (WHOI); Helena McMonagle, graduate student, University of Washington; Kayla Gardner, PhD student, MIT-WHOI joint program; and Michelle's friend Cedric, a freediving instructor. Any errors that remain are our own.

Published by Charlesbridge
9 Galen Street, Watertown, MA 02472
(617) 926-0329 • www.charlesbridge.com

Library of Congress Cataloging-in-Publication Data
Names: Cusolito, Michelle, author. | Wong, Nicole (Nicole E.), illustrator.
Title: Diving deep: using machines to explore the ocean /Michelle Cusolito; illustrated by Nicole Wong.
Description: Watertown, Massachusetts: Charlesbridge, [2022] | Audience: Ages 5–9 years | Audience: Grades 2–3 | Summary: "Humans use machines to explore the ocean—from snorkel gear to submersibles—and they ask, 'How deep can we dive?'"—Provided by publisher.
Identifiers: LCCN 2021013264 (print) | LCCN 2021013265 (ebook) | ISBN 9781623542931 (Hardcover) | ISBN 9781632899286 (eBook)
Subjects: LCSH: Underwater exploration—Juvenile literature. | Oceanography—Juvenile literature. | Skin diving—Juvenile literature. | Scuba diving—Juvenile literature. | Saturation diving—Juvenile literature. | Deep diving—Equipment and supplies. | Submersibles—Juvenile literature.
Classification: LCC GC65 .C87 2022 (print) | LCC GC65 (ebook) | DDC 551.46—dc23
LC record available at https://lccn.loc.gov/2021013264
LC ebook record available at https://lccn.loc.gov/2021013265

Printed in China
(hc) 10 9 8 7 6 5 4 3 2 1

Illustrations created digitally on the iPad using the Procreate app
Display type set in Rabbits by Typetype
Text type set in Mikado by Hannes von Doehren
Color separations and printing by 1010 Printing International Limited in Huizhou, Guangdong, China
Production supervision by Jennifer Most Delaney
Designed by Diane M. Earley

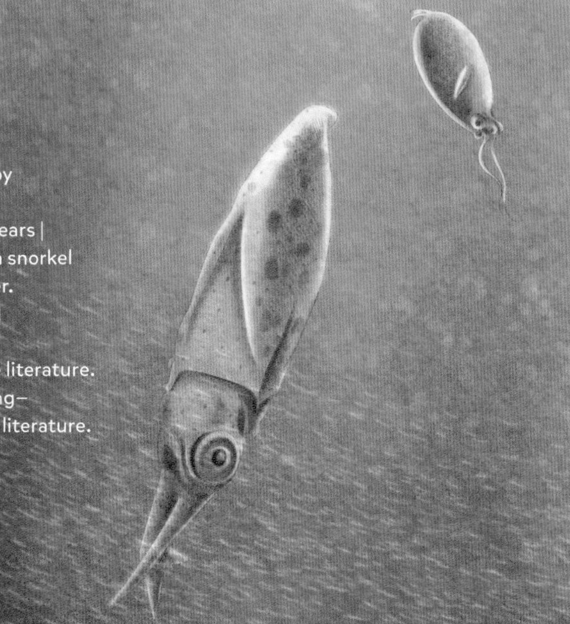